BENEDICT RUBBRA

PAINTINGS 1958–1998

BENEDICT RUBBRA

PAINTINGS 1958–1998

Ideas and influences

This book has been published to coincide with the

SIXTIETH BIRTHDAY RETROSPECTIVE EXHIBITION

of the work of Benedict Rubbra

at the Buckinghamshire Art Gallery and County Museum, Aylesbury

18 April –14 June 1998

ACKNOWLEDGEMENTS

I was encouraged to produce this book by Brenda Herbert who gave me sound advice about how it should be published, and then edited the text. I am deeply grateful also to Carol Graham, Sir Bryan Cartledge and Jonathan Turner for their contributions to the text, and to Gillian Greenwood for designing the book, and to the owners of paintings that have either been bought or commissioned, for permission to reproduce them here. Above all, my deepest gratitude is to Tessa for her guidance and invaluable suggestions as the book progressed.

Finally, my true appreciation to The Finzi Trust for their generosity towards the cost of this publication, and to Hamilton Colour (High Wycombe) for donating the cost of processing photographs and transparencies for the illustrations.

I will always treasure the encouragement and help that all my friends and my family have given me over the years.

© Benedict Rubbra 1998
First published in 1998 by Benedict Rubbra, Valley Cottage, Speen, Bucks HP27 0PY

ISBN 0 9531894 0 6

Designed by Gillian Greenwood
Printed and bound in Italy by Grafiche Milani

HALF TITLE The model for *Singing blackbird*. Light directed onto painted card
TITLE PAGE Benedict with the model for *Bluebell Wood*. Photo Marianne Majerus
COVER *An orange grove*

CONTENTS

The garden gate
Gouache and ink on paper

21.4.96.

I have been looking at Ben Rubbra's paintings over a period of thirty-four years, following changes in the work of this most thoughtful and sensitive artist.

After the early production of landscapes and still life of a figurative nature, and the commencement of a professional career as a portrait painter, his work began to take on a highly individual quality whereby he looked at the natural world around him and transmuted it by an intellectual process into its elemental parts, thus giving it cosmic significance. He did this by concentrating on the nature of what he was looking at, then expressing its essential qualities in universal terms so that the subject matter became a metaphor, and his paintings began to take on visionary qualities: a metaphor linked with growth, the seasons, night and day, the intrinsic nature of places. I remember using the term 'organic abstractions' because Ben's paintings consisted of shapes and tones unrelated to the natural world as we know it, yet strongly suggestive of it and imbuing them with greater significance because of his rearrangement and presentation of them. His construct heightened their innate natures, yet they are not present in the form we usually know them by, and his imposition of an idiosyncratic order underlies their vital role and nature.

Whether it is the pale unfolding of hidden flowers in winter sunshine, the delicacy of an opening seed pod [page 60], the radiance of stained glass on worn mediaeval stone [page 64], or a violent and turbid synthesis of a Spanish experience [page 47] – all phenomena have been observed, absorbed, reconstructed and represented in a way that makes us even more poignantly aware of their momentousness.

The fact that what is naturalistic is interpreted by coils and discs of paper, blocks of plaster, tissue, light and paint, manipulated with infinite discipline yet miraculously suggestive of growth, life, movement of an even greater intensity is one of the most impressive aspects of his work.

There is a painting based on a visit to the south-eastern Peloponnese: the background consists of thick, wavy, striated bars of olive, orange and blue flowing transversely across the surface (perhaps tree, rock and sky). Projected on this is a worked orange square on which three-dimensional fragments of a softer, brighter, or duller similar colour are displayed in relationship to each other, Some are rolls of paper with large perforations encouraging intriguing shadows; others are pale and fragile discs, or knotted coils with sombre declivities. The sharp contrast of tone evoking light and shade, the dry hot colours, the fragments themselves are highly suggestive of both the landscape of Greece and the archaic, infinitely complex and convoluted history and culture of its people.

Another earlier, fascinating painting is about olive trees in Tuscany: it consists of meticulous squares of thousands of little leaf-shaped dabs of paint in a glorious medley of leaf-colours amassed to give a sensation of receding and advancing planes. Superimposed across the background is an

Landscape in Northern Italy
Pencil on paper

opened, angled screen of more squares, but this time at their centre are the trees themselves, with their Homeric many-eyed trunks, twisted and whorled, holding up out-flung arms in a more intensive storm of their tinier leaves. These whirl around and about in reticulations that emphasise the subtle planes of each square. The very essence of the olive grove is captured here – the heavy, knotted branches distorted with age, dark in a mottled cloud of dappled light and shade. Yet this is a highly disciplined construction, dependent for its effect on squares, horizontals and verticals, receding and oncoming planes and thousands of tiny dabs of paint.

As time passes Ben Rubbra's work seems to become more and more imbued with cosmographic forces: the earth's rotation, the process of maturation; the movement of the waters, the mystery of light, bird-song; and as these are huge subjects the necessary discipline involved in transmogifying them on to canvas or paper is considerable.

The subject is viewed, thought about and then brought under control by very exact and careful drawing, during which it goes through a complicated intellectual screening; then scrupulous models are made from the drawing with paper, cardboard, tissues, spirals, cut and slashed paper. These are arranged with special lighting effects before any painting of the picture itself is undertaken. Thus the subject matter in hand has gone through diverse processes of observation, duplication, absorption, and replication so that when it is presented to us it is the end result of a great deal of both sensory and cognitive awareness.

The other element that has become more and more apparent has been the increased photism of his paintings: a sense of light comparable to some of Howard Hodgkin's work; we feel that they could glow in the dark, whether we are being shown ripening apples on a sunlit tree, a golden church in Siena, a Tuscan landscape, or Zeus's shower of gold.

A life spent in a much-loved and beautiful part of the Chilterns with tumbling grass hills and beech-wood ridges, together with regular visits to Fiesole, have given him a strong consciousness of contrasting kinds of light and its transforming quality. In fact such a background has been a matrix to his awareness of the elemental grandeur of the natural world and his lyrical interpretation of it. Clearing woodland in spring, collecting autumn 'fallers' from apple trees, closing down hens under night sky or shifting snow in a lane are all good solid groundwork for such consummate appreciation.

He himself wrote, 'The problem of seeing what we know and what we think we know must be considered very seriously'. The whole of his working life has been devoted to trying to find a painterly solution to this puzzle in universal terms.

Carol Graham 1998

My lifetime – I was born in 1937 – has been a time of great experimentation in the plastic arts as it has been in all the branches of art which convention has established.

It is all too easy to be glib about this; the sequence and cluster of schools and ideologies, many of which make use of the suffix 'ism' in their titles, provide many a 'happy hunting ground' for the slightest lecturer, and for the wordy student.

But just as, when beginning studies and practice, students desperately want to be sure that they are cultivating fruitful ground – and I recall 'our days' as students – so it is at a later stage. With great determination one wants to to be sure that one is not dealing in nonsense.

Where Benedict is concerned my mind is happily at rest. Artists make statements and write, and Benedict stands firmly behind what he says and writes, but most importantly, in his paintings there is no falsity, no nonsense in evidence. This is more of an achievement than is at first apparent in an era of such thoroughgoing experimentation. But thought and action have come together – are integrated – in his work.

Art, said Manet, is *une bagarre*, a fight or a struggle, and one in which, he says, 'your skin is at stake', *il faut y mettre la peau*. Great determination is required, and the strongest feelings must be subordinated to that determination. These paintings, and his other works reveal that quality also.

Benedict's modus operandi is quite extraordinary: many modern painters are preoccupied with surface. The Bauhaus books, such as Wassily Kandinsky's *Concerning the Spiritual in Art*, and *Point and Line and Surface*, give insight into the surfaces, the formats, and their complexities. And the painting surface must always retain our interest, involve us, and involve our feeling. What is more, if it is to be of the quality for which we hope, it must do these things with increasing interest over a period of years. I believe that Benedict's paintings will do so and it is a matter for celebration.

I don't know enough – and I won't ever know enough, I think – about the evolution of Benedict's solution to that utterly fascinating problem of composition of paintings. For the present we note that, just as Nicholas Poussin evolved models from which to make studies – on a stage with scenery constructed as, for example, a landscape and accompanying figures clothed with fragments of cloth, so Ernst Gombrich told us – so does Benedict. But he lights his models with modern technology rather than Poussin's dusky candles.

This process and this solution enable Benedict, with all before him prepared to his satisfaction and to the highest standard, to work absorbedly with brush, with palette, and with the surface of the canvas.

The Constructivist artist Kenneth Martin would talk to his students at Goldsmith's and the Slade School about the 'shed' to be found in Poussin's work. 'Shed' is a term in weaving. It means the space through which the

A model prepared for a painting. Wood and card

9

shuttle glides to and fro. One may see what is meant when comparing two magnificent National Gallery Poussins, *The Adoration of the Golden Calf* and *A Bacchanalian Revel*, one painting being in part the mirror image of the other. Benedict too, is weaving. Undoubtedly many passages are lyrical and some are magical.

Jonathan Turner 1998

A nest in the centre
Oil on canvas

IDEAS AND INFLUENCES

The mind is the real instrument of sight and observation. The eye acts as a sort of vessel receiving and transmitting the visible portion of the consciousness.   PLINY

The environment that I was born into seemed to be timeless, making it difficult to imagine that it had a beginning or would ever have an end. I imagined the perspective of the fields continuing for ever beyond the horizon of the rounded hill that faced our house and the surrounding beech woods seemed incomprehensibly deep. Placed within this space was our flint and brick cottage. It lay in a long V-shaped valley, and two hills, one behind and one in front, were like two walls. The cottage was a home within a home and it became a point that I could relate to within the centre of this seemingly measureless space. Even now, my response, through painting, is to try to recreate and then substantiate this space. I need to find out where the edges are. However, the mystery of being in a space with no end or beginning will always remain within me.

There are many ways that we can express the instinct to define and control these edges, perhaps the edges of our territory. Stone circles, as markers, are made in a wild landscape, or a dancer will move legs, body and arms to explore the limits of his or her space. My instinct is to let the edges of the canvas or the paper symbolise the limits of my environment. The centre of the page becomes my home, my eye, and is always the starting point for a drawing or painting.

A BEGINNING

Young orange tree grown from a pip.

The actual process of drawing can spark off an uncanny thrill and I remember this happening for the first time. Drawing a young orange tree in a pot, a plant that I had grown from a pip, I managed, by putting one leaf behind another, to make a space of my own. I drew a cat half hidden by the arm of a chair. Spaces were made in which I was free to move. Later I went

A cat half hidden by the arm of a chair.

COMMON MALLOW

MALVA SYLVESTRIS

out into the fields on either side of the valley to collect wild flowers to draw. The space around me seemed to extend not only outwards, but downwards into the earth. Under the topsoil there was a harsh mixture of clay, chalk and flint, and at the time that I was drawing my orange tree I was learning how to garden. In the first letter sent to me when I was away at boarding school, my mother wrote, 'I am taking great care of your garden. Your beans are wonderful and also the lettuces. I shall soon be able to transplant them!' My ties with home were kept alive by imagining these new plants growing and making their own space. Many years later I painted a bursting seed pod [page 60]. I wanted to express the idea that all forms of life need their own particular environment in which to develop. A pod bursts and the seeds spread outwards, sometimes beyond their known territory.

The garden has now become a symbol for continuity, regeneration and creation. It excites me to know that withered plants are transformed into new black earth and that new organic forms are nourished by a plasma that is made from this decayed life. I can see fruit buds forming for next year on the branches of the newly planted apple trees and all around me there is a pulse that moves, repeating relentlessly, yet following a circular form. I wrote in my note book:

I am excited by a continuous movement as each season prepares for the next.
The shortest day is dark and yet it gives more hope than the longest day that is
saturated with light. I feel the potential growth in waiting seeds and am part of the
increasing momentum of light. The shortest day expresses the frailty that is
in all beginnings, and yet it must have the strength to sustain the year ahead.
There is a rhythm of continuity.

Often, as with a seed, an idea for a painting lies dormant for several years and I have learnt that one cannot force the realisation of an idea if the time or climate is not right. A few years ago areas of dense undergrowth were cleared from our woodland to let light penetrate the ground. Robust primroses appeared that had been waiting many years for their moment to flower. The jotting in my notebook continues:

I have to let myself be dictated to by nature. It calls the tune and beats the
rhythms. In the natural world complex survival mechanisms are developed. Seeds
are designed to travel over great distances and insects to change colour. If I am able
to relate my pace of life to the pace of the growth sequences and patterns of plants,
then I will have achieved something.

Ideas will often arrive unexpectedly, stimulated perhaps by movements of birds or insects or light passing through trees. Impressions are noted, then wait to be reformed into a painting. One late summer evening I wrote:

A curtain of dark green ash leaves hide a yellow evening sky that I know will be reinstated by the morning sun. The evening sun spotlighting the formal patterns of insects. The warmth of the sun activating their dance against the dropping sun. A dance in an organised volume of light.

I continued: 'Birds drawing in the sky. Birds describing sounds in a space. Far away the cry of a magpie is like a scratch in the sky. The landscape is prised open with the song of birds, each note marking points on the outer edges of the air'. Another evening I noticed the rhythmic swaying and sweeping of ash branches heavy with leaves and I remembered hearing the *Spem in Alium* of Tallis. How, I wondered, could these musical sweeps be made into a painting.

I wrote, ten years before I painted *Picking blackcurrants* [page 56]:

Today I crushed blackcurrants for wine. The smell in the fruit cage was like rich raspberry jam. A picture is forming of rich purples and reds in a surround of warmth, maturity. Does the form of a painting begin to appear when the dynamic relationship between the birth of an idea, its metamorphosis and the observer is established?

An evening dance
From a sketch book.

Birdsong in a landscape
From a sketchbook.

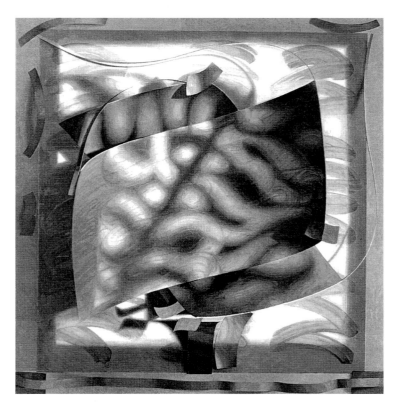

A sunlit tree
Inspired by *Spem in Alium*.

SCHOOL

Nell Todd
with Ben at Christ's Hospital.

On the sports field.

My first school was at Piggots, a little hamlet surrounded by beech woods. Sometimes I walked to school carrying my soup in a blue enamelled can. A path led me through an ancient wood in the centre of which was a black pond that frightened me. The spirit of Eric Gill, who lived and worked at Piggots, was everywhere. Peering at me round every corner were smooth-lined figures emerging from pieces of stone and on the school walls were delicate watercolours by David Jones. The classroom took up one side of a closed-in grass courtyard and in the centre was a pig-sty. Sometimes lessons were interrupted with the desperate sound of an animal being slaughtered.

From Piggots I went to the local village school in Speen and then, when I was nine, to Christ's Hospital. Two years passed and then the new art teacher arrived and immediately I had a friend and a teacher who helped and inspired me through the rest of my school days. She talked passionately about colour and I loved her large free canvases.

Nell Todd is showing paintings which might be called expressionist/ impressionist, since her aim seems to be to capture visual pleasure in landscape experiences, while her method is that of Monet. THE TIMES

Nell Todd is a bold decorator who works in a broad manner that reminds you of late period Monet spiced with a dash of Bonnard's sharper vision. THE SCOTSMAN

Nell kept chickens in the Art School, and in the summer the room was full of the scent and colours of lilac and peonies, roses and laburnum and rhododendrons. On Speech Days she wore gorgeous hats. I helped her make one, decorated with birds nests and fruit. I tried to paint her portrait. I wrote home:

The portrait I did of Nell was really a study. A study for the plains and tones. Nell's face is absolutely impossible to paint, so consequently it is not quite finished. Miss Todd only looks herself when she puts on her hundred and one facial expressions and when I tell her to keep still, it looks nothing like her. Can you understand what I mean?

Sometimes there was a conflict with time spent on the sports field and time spent in the art school. One school report said: 'A real sense of poetry in some of his paintings. It is a pity he does not paint more in his spare time.' But during my last two years I spent all my time in the Art School, except for a day a week at Camberwell School of Art, where I went to learn life drawing. I wrote home, 'Today was the last day at Camberwell. Thank goodness! The journey takes two hours from door to door. I have only ten minutes tuition. I began to draw my own drawings and not art school ones. This start will be a great help at the Slade.'

I left Christ's Hospital armed with Nell's loving confidence but when I arrived at the Slade I knew that all my adolescent passions about painting had to be quelled. I needed time to think, and it was through the structured lessons given by Patrick George that the beginnings of a new direction were found. I began to experience the thrill of concentrating and training the eye to select and look for relationships of form and line. In his painting classes we had in front of us groups of forms, all painted white, and we were made to find colour and tone relationships. Preconceived ideas were stripped away and for the first time my eyes began to work.

The sense of sight discerns the different shapes, whatever they are, without delay or interruption, making careful calculations with almost incredible skill, yet acting unnoticed because of its speed. When the sense cannot see the object through its own mode of action, it recognises it through the manifestation of other differences, sometimes perceiving truly and sometimes imagining incorrectly.

PTOLEMY

Wells Cathedral
A spacious interior.

15

I needed this ordered, structured approach to painting and drawing and I began to understand how I could to use it as a point of departure. In the spacious painting studios were other students, seemingly confident, with huge tins of paint from Brodie and Middleton at the base of their easels. Wide brushes slashed diagonally and up and down and across the canvas, paint dripping, paint everywhere. These large Bomberg style paintings were full of rich earth colours and textures and sometimes it was difficult to distinguish the difference between the canvas and the painter's rags and clothes.

During weekends I came back home to work in my new studio. It stood half way up a steep slope and a large window framed the view of the hill opposite and the valley and the cottage below. I noticed the relationship of the window frame to the space outside and the sensation of being both inside and outside has continued to interest me. I recognise it in the spacious interiors of cathedrals [page 15] and in the beech woods nearby.

As a fact of pure experience, there is no space without time, no time without space. They are interpenetrating.

Music is an expression of being in sequence with life because it divides, measures and articulates time. Music is linear, in the sense that it has a marked beginning and a marked end. These limits, or edges, (the fixed points within which one is free to work) are established by a time element. There is no time element associated with drawing and painting – but the spatial qualities of music and painting are nevertheless similar. With music the spacial quality is formed by the layering of sounds and rhythms reacting to each other on different levels; with painting it is by the layering of shapes and colours.

The layers of sounds and rhythms in music take us, predominately, deep into a space. My eye, as it progresses through layers of colour and form, is taken behind the surface of the canvas. I want the eye to go back into the canvas rather than move from side to side.

The screen print *Winter sunlight sarching for snowdrops* originated from a construction that was deliberately built up in layers. The first layer was made of swirling shapes like the swirling 'skirt' of the snowdrop. I then added to the surface 18 identical sharp paper shapes (like new white teeth pushing up through the earth). Rings of paper were suspended from these sharp shapes. Finally I directed a strong light, through holes in a screen, onto the construction.

Winter sunlight searching for snowdrops.

A sketch of my mother practising her violin.

My mother with her violin.

My mother was a violinist. She used to tell me how she had to practice standing on a stool to be out of reach of my hand disturbing her bowing arm. She would walk up and down the room, eyes closed, passionately engrossed in the Bach Chaconne (from the Partita No.2 for unaccompanied violin) or her rich full tone would articulate the rocking and swaying of the sonata by Franck. In the early morning I remember floating into consciousness with the sound of my father Edmund Rubbra practising the Schubert B flat and Ravel trios. Ribbons of sound filtered up through the gaps of the floor boards. I have often used the image of the ribbon as a metaphor for a continuous forward movement in time.

Often musicians would come to Valley Cottage to rehearse my father's new compositions. I remember the excitement of hearing The Griller Quartet, the viola of William Primrose and the cello of William Pleeth. Through Vaughan Williams my parents became close friends of Gerald and Joy Finzi.

I took my violin to school and nervously took part in solo music competitions (one year my father was the adjudicator) but I played in the orchestra with more confidence. I would write home:

The orchestra played the Barber of Seville overture. This is really hard and in a key with four sharps. A younger member of the orchestra was asked by a master how he coped with such a difficult key. Oh, he replied, I don't worry about sharps. I have to concentrate on the notes.

18

A letter would arrive from my mother: 'Barbirolli conducted the 6th like an angel in a concert at Oxford last night.' A little later I wrote to my father, 'I heard your 6th symphony on the radio. Every time I hear the slow movement I weep with the beauty of it. I am sure it is the most beautiful piece of music ever written.'

Through hearing my mother repeating and repeating a phrase until the sounds felt right, I learnt the importance of the discipline of practice. Drawing can sometimes be treated like the practice of a musical scale. The discipline is to select and then concentrate on one particular event that is happening to a line or to a tone or a shape. I wrote a piece about the discipline of drawing:

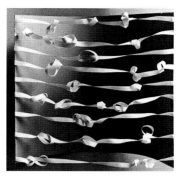

Ribbons of sound
A model with strips of knotted paper.

Let the point of the pencil be your eye that follows lines. Let the point of the pencil speak as it describes the form that it is walking over. You are living in a space and the eye is the centre and you are surrounded by a complexity of hidden lines. Somewhere there are lines that wrap up shapes, lines that flow forward as a river, lines that push the eye backward and forward and from side to side. These lines can be discovered and then rephrased by searching for the contour of a shape or for the rhythms that join up the accents that lie within and on the forms. Search for a

My father practising in the early morning.

19

*conversation between relative directions and movements and the surrounding
muddle is put into some sort of order. It must be clear inside the eye what the eye
is to select. We must 'see' something happening and when a line has been
discovered and its character selected then it is possible to draw a line that is sure in
its message. The meaning of the message becomes clear when the relationships
between the lines are found. One single line on paper has no meaning. Its meaning
only appears as another line is drawn and a relationship is established.*

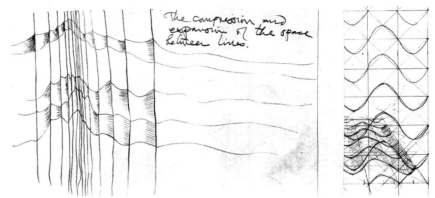

The compression and expansion of the space between lines. From a sketch book.

Through my father I experienced the agonies that he went through trying to create, that is, starting something from nothing. I became familiar with
his particular process of composing. At lunch time he would come down
from his studio, at the top of the hill above the cottage, and sing a composed
phrase, or just a bar, against shapes of chords on the piano. These would be
analysed with my mother and the excitements and difficulties discussed.
Some mornings nothing would fit. He destroyed the good bits that were
preventing the forward movement. He wrote, and this interests me in rela-
tion to the finding of a beginning and an end: 'The movement that I have
completed of the 6th symphony is now the last movement and I am now
working on the first, actually originally intended for the last movement.
This change in order is, musically, far better and gets rid of the technical difficulty of beginning with a cor anglais solo, before the player has had time
to warm up his instument.'

Working on a portrait of my father.

At the end of my father's life, when I was painting his portrait, I talked with him about methods of work. I remember discussing the problem of controlling one's work and at the same time letting it develop freely. We agreed that an idea, or cell, when secure, will unfold and develop with its own energy. The idea will become the space in which one can freely think and work.

The idea for *Bluebell Wood* [page 48] came soon after listening to the recording sessions of my father's Violin and Viola Concertos. Vernon Handley was conducting the Royal Philharmonic Orchestra. Tasmin Little played the violin and Rivka Golani the viola. The idea, or cell, of the painting was inspired by the inner strength and controlled tension of the music. I began to make a three-dimensional construction out of coloured card and paper that was to be the space from which the painting would develop. (The Fibonacci series 1.1.2.3.5.8.13.21.34.... was used as the basis for the geometry and harmony.) The blues and greens of an English landscape weave in and out of the columns of the trees that are both the main structure and the repeated pulses of sound. Sudden bursts of light, like colourful sounds, are directed onto the construction and punctuate the space. The light alters the colour of the dominant forms as a shift in key alters the spirit of the musical structure. When the distribution of the light onto the colours and forms of the construction were completed, I painted it as if it was a landscape. I painted the form that I had made. I looked at myself, as Edmund looked at himself when he listened to the music that he had written.

Paintings and prints by Benedict Rubbra.

The Chapter House, Wells Cathedral. Working Model.

You are cordially invited to the
1994 Exhibition
of Paintings, Prints, Pottery, at
The Studio and Pottery.

Monday 20 June.
Every day from 12 noon to 6 pm.
The exhibition continues until
Sunday 3 July.

The Studio and Pottery, Speen,
Princes Risborough, Bucks.
Enquiries. (0494) 488 206

Pottery by Tessa Rubbra.

Three Striped Jugs.   *(cover) Striped Jug and dinner plate*

EXHIBITIONS AT VALLEY COTTAGE

In 1964 Tessa and I married, and we lived for our first year in one large room in Chiswick. I began to paint this room that was my world. I wrote in my sketch book:

Mantelpiece and mirror. Movement of vision. The impact of entering a room. Not involved with the logical recessions of spatial shapes. One cannot be logical about space because vision is not logical. It depends on mood and temperament. Problem: To paint a space that one can be involved in rather than a space that is just static. One must become involved in the picture. In this way one is part of the space.

I was trying to interpret the seemingly chaotic shapes and lines around me and I was frightened that I would see the room not objectively, but in terms of the style that I was developing. During this period I had an exhibition at the Woodstock Gallery in London. The critic from *The Times* wrote: 'Benedict Rubbra's paintings vacillate considerably between the obvious struggle for and realisation of his vision.' I painted large canvases of interiors relating to the shapes and spaces that I saw outside [page 39].

We then moved upstairs to a larger flat, full of light. One of the rooms became my studio and I began to introduce spherical objects into it. Wooden balls would hang from the ceiling and oranges were randomly placed on the floor or table. The whole space was filled and the eye moved from one similar form to another [page 40]. I wanted my eye to travel over as large a space as possible. Vertical and horizontal lines would perpetually change direction as the eye moved up and down and across. I was beginning the

22

idea of making a space that I could enter. I was making and then painting my own space. Some time later, at Valley Cottage (Tessa and I had left London), I began building, brick by brick, my own studio. It was gruelling but satisfying work. Tobias was born before the building began and two and a half years later we had our second child, Tabitha. Tessa taught me how to maintain a balance between keeping a family and devoting time to painting.

Ten years later, when the children were at school during the day, Tessa was able to work full time in her pottery. An annex to the cottage had been converted into a workshop and Speen Pottery was established. We soon discovered that we were sharing methods for working. Tessa would cut out shapes from thin paper and designs would gradually be resolved as each shape was placed and then replaced on the beautiful leather-hard unfired pots. At the same time, in my studio at the opposite end of the house, I would be resolving a form by the distribution of coloured paper shapes, the

Benedict and Tessa with Tobias and Tabitha in front of the newly built studio.

23

The hills of Anticoli Corrado
Pencil on paper.

colours often inspired by the clarity and harmony that I saw on her newly fired pots. Sometimes I would be called to the Pottery to untangle a design problem; or I would ask Tessa to look at a painting that was losing its sense of direction. Invariably she had the special ability to pinpoint the area of colour or tone that was preventing the resolution of the painting.

I designed the new studio as a space for work and for exhibitions. These were held every two years in the summer starting in 1970. Tessa displayed her pots and I showed paintings and drawings and commissioned portraits, all completed since the previous exhibition. The year of the exhibition gave a special focus to our work. Months of preparation, from the design of the invitation card to the refurbishing of the studio and workshop were carefully planned and as the Private View drew near we anxiously studied the weather maps, hoping for a fine day. The family helped to prepare the food and wine and a splendid lunch was spread out on tables in the garden. Lots of people came and sales were made and we were, and still are, indebted to all our friends for their support and enthusiasm. But it was Joy Finzi who would always arrive the day before the exhibition began determined to buy one, sometimes two, paintings or drawings. She became closely involved in my work and I valued profoundly her commitment and encouragement. On 12 June 1981 she wrote to me, 'it was an exciting exhibition and the whole home prepared for it so adds to the general impression of quality. As usual I find your work very stimulating and there are several paintings that I would have gladly removed from the walls and I am very excited at the thought of *Turbulence* finding its way to somewhere on these walls. Two others remain clearly in mind – *The breeze caressing stones and water* and, persistently, *Italian sunset*. All these drawings seem to have so much colour!'

24

My mother's family were French but lived in Italy in a beautiful villa at the foot of Fiesole just outside Florence. When I was nine I went with my mother to visit my grandmother and aunt. This first taste of Italy made a deep impression on me. My aunt Elizabeth was a painter (there is a room of her work at the Palazzo Pitti in Florence) and she gave me her paint box. I am still using it. In her studio the summer heat intensified the heady smell of oil and turpentine and I was spellbound by her skill in picking up such rich and apt colours with her large brushes. The studio was above the *cantina* where olives and grapes were crushed, and in the orchard two white oxen ploughed between the olive trees and vines. From the roof terrace I saw the three hills of Fiesole and the monastery at San Domenico where Fra Angelico worked before moving to San Marco. His paintings echoed perfectly this landscape of pure colour and clear contour, and even the taste of the sweet basil from the garden below, where later I painted my first picture out in the open [page 38],` helped to complete this harmony.

Many influential visits to Italy followed. I wrote: 'Venice, August 1952. We saw a terrific statue of a horse and warrior by Verrochio. It has poise, power and beauty … the afternoon was spent wandering about this dream town. I wish I could stay here all my life.'

I saw the paintings of Giotto for the first time. 'Had lunch and saw what I think are the most beautiful frescoes that could have been painted. The whole chapel, painted entirely by him, had a wonderful unity. He used

Two white oxen ploughing.

25

wonderfully simple colours. The paintings have a wonderful rhythm, got by the use of drapery on the people. The backs of his people are wonderful.' My father was also moved by the frescoes. I found in his diary, written at the same time: '… to see the Giotto. Spent three hours there viewing the marvel. Never perhaps has simplicity (a Mozartian simplicity that hides the powerful technique) and deep feeling been wedded to such purpose.'

The holidays were over and I was back at school. I wrote:

Memories of sunny Italy are always with me. Today I began a painting of the Florentine landscape. Dark twisted olives with silvery green leaves set against rich red soil … I am transported amongst the oxen, vines and olives …'

Santa Maria degli Innocenti, Florence.

The charioteer at Delphi. From a sketch book.

Brunelleschi and Fra Angelico are two Florentine artists that I need to return to time and time again. The harmony of the inner courtyard of the Spedale di Santa Maria degli Innocenti, and the controlled vigour of the Pazzi Chapel, both designed by Brunelleschi, and the timeless purity of Fra Angelico continually inspire me.

The prospect of travelling abroad continued to excite me and I was fortunate, after graduating at the Slade School, to have the opportunity of visiting Greece. There I saw a new landscape of brilliant, clear colours and the perfection of balance of form and emotion in the marble and bronze statues seemed to relate to the works of Brunelleschi and Fra Angelico.

26

The charioteer was alive. His feet parallel and his body slightly tipping as if the chariot was turning a corner. His bent arm holding the reins was modelled in the most subtle way and I felt that his arm must be aching.

(Written in my sketch book, 1961).

I became interested in the ancient Greek legends and how they expressed, in symbolic terms, our relationship to nature and the landscape. There is the legend of the attraction of Zeus to Danae. She was locked in an underground room built of bronze and Zeus came to her disguised as a shower of gold and Perseus was born. I see the shower of gold as the symbol for sunlight penetrating the earth and germinating the seed. At this point I began to think that

it would be possible to interpret a landscape in terms of symbols made from abstract shapes cut out of paper.

A Greek legend
Oil on canvas.

From Greece I went to France. I camped for a month in a field at Le Tholonet outside Aix-en-Provence. I painted six canvases of the red earth and dark green pines [page 28]. Inevitably, every day was dominated by Mont Saint-Victoire and the timeless strength of Cezanne. It was here I experienced for the first time some of the practical hazards of painting outside. I wrote home: 'The scirocco began suddenly yesterday and I rigged up a most fantastic display of rope going from the canvas and easel round trees, roots and stones, and it worked!' Some years later I revisited the spot where I held

Landscape near Aix-en-Provence
Oil on canvas.

down my easel with ropes. My hardened colours and the top of a paint tube were still visible.

This month of concentrated work was an important time for me. I confronted for the first time the problem of finding points in the landscape that would relate to the edge of the canvas. It seemed an arbitrary task because the essence of being in a landscape is involvement in the total space rather than involvement with an arbitrary section of it. The only fixed point was where I stood.

Many years later I wrote:

There can be no fixed point. As I move in a landscape shapes between the sky and the ground change. The landscape can only be understood using a thousand eyes from a thousand different places. It is exciting to see the sky under a tree, but if I turn my head the sky is somewhere else or the tree is somewhere else, or am I somewhere else?

I also wrote, later still: 'An accurate drawing of a tree by its very nature cannot be accurate because it is described precisely from only one viewpoint', and I thought about Mallarmé's dictum: *The artist is concerned not with the thing, but with the effect that it produces.*

28

The skies yet blushing with departing light,
When falling dew with spangles deck'd the glade,
And the low sun has lengthened every shade.

Alexander Pope, from *The Third Pastoral, Autumn*

THE INFLUENCE OF LIGHT

Light poured in from the large window of my new studio. In our valley the sun arrives late and sets early. The first rays of light run parallel with the ground forming shapes on the ground that change within seconds. In the evening the same slope, with the sunlight directed on it fully, has become a different hill. A crab apple tree fragmented by the morning sun has become solid in the evening light.

The concept that light transforms the subject is central to my work. Many years ago I wrote home from school: 'This morning I saw something really wonderful. It was all the sparkling frost on silvery birches intermingled with fog. In the background was the thick smoke of a train made golden by the sun breaking its way through the fog .'

A photographic study of evening light.

Self portrait
Pencil on torn and
reassembled paper.

And recently I went to Bourges. The windows of the cathedral, seen from the outside, were dull grey and lifeless and yet seen from the inside these same windows were a blazing wealth of colour. I was intrigued with the idea that one entity could be transformed by the direction and density of the light [page 64].

My new studio was full of light from outside but I looked into my studio and into my work. I began to make drawings from my own paintings. Sometimes I would cut up and then reform drawings. I began to make the subject that I would then paint. I made paintings of crumpled paper and then superimposed drawings, transferred from sketch books, onto these textured surfaces, sometimes adding 'drawn' lines made with strips of paper. Paintings on card were sliced so that I could bend sections forward and backward to let light enter from behind. Coloured tissue paper was placed over the cuts, diffusing the light and so transforming the lines into unexpected directions and complexions . With *Autumn* [page 32] I used two directions of light for the first time; the area of filtered light was also being gently lit from the side.

I soon realised that, by using a powerful spotlight, the shapes that I had made could be reformed by directing the light either at different angles or through shaped screens, and, by varying the quality and direction of light, different paintings could be made from the same model. I discovered that I was able to 'draw' with light and that light would reshape and extend surfaces as the sun would do as it shifted behind a cloud or sank below the horizon. New colours would be revealed by changing the intensity and disposition of the light. It excited me to know that a particular colour that I had chosen to put on a surface would unexpectedly change its character when a strong light was projected on it. I knew what the colour should be but I was seeing something entirely different.

A model of crumpled cloth.

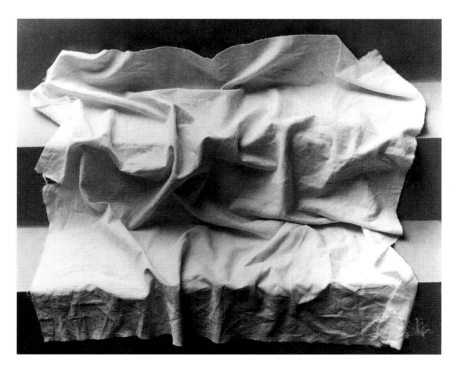

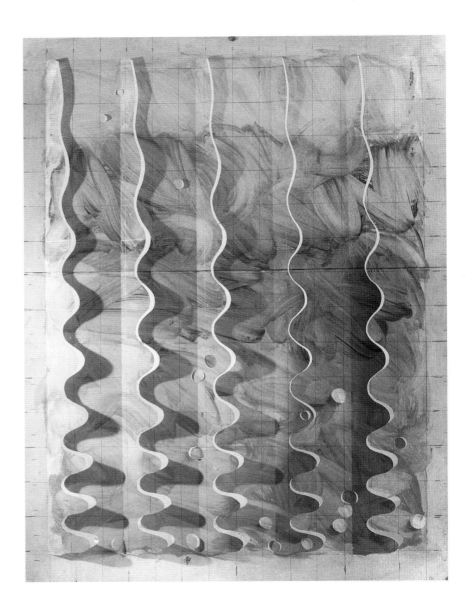

Model for *Autumn* showing two directions of light.

There is a magic element in light that can change at will the form and mood of colour, and this drew me to the idea that I could use light as a medium to express transience. I am interested in significant moments that can hardly be measured or the moment that is expected but has passed without being noticed, like the change from winter to spring.

32

*I feel a surge of electricity in the space
between the two gentle figures.
The vital power that exists between two thoughts.*

A sketch of the
Botticelli *Annunciation*.

The model for *The Annunciation*.
Light shining through cut shapes
and tissue paper.

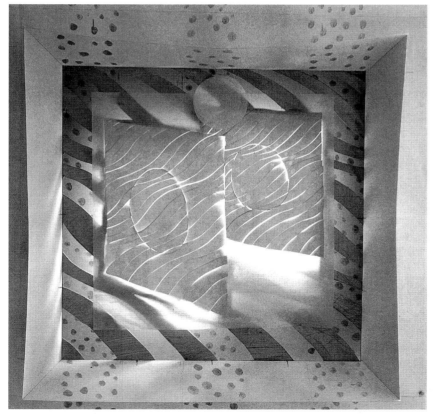

Oh! how this spring of love resembleth
The uncertain glory of an April day
Which now shows all the beauty of the sun
And by and by a cloud takes all away .

William Shakespeare
Two Gentlemen of Verona

April clouds. Pencil on paper.

The reaction of light on water produces continually moving and changing shapes and colours. In the summer of 1980 we took a family holiday on the island of Eigg, off the west coast of Scotland. Water was everywhere. I made drawings and photographic studies of the movement of water in the sea and in mountain streams. I was fascinated by the inevitable yet unnoticed shift from one colour or form to another, a shift that Sibelius expresses so well in music, and it intrigued me that, visually, the essence and complexion of the water was destroyed when fixed in a still photographic form.

I continually invent new techniques and ideas for the construction of the models. Some are constructed with solid materials such as wood, cloth and plaster and thicker card, and often, to maintain a sense of continuity, a coloured shape or a piece of wood [see page 70 *Venice* and page 66 *Water flowing through trees*] is re-used. The colour is distributed by placing and shifting and then fixing shapes of painted paper. Each model is designed to be seen from one precise viewpoint. This fixed position (my eye is the centre of the space) must be kept constant as I am always aware how perceptions can vary according to the position of this viewpoint.

The design of each construction has always developed from a very simple form based on a circle and the geometric divisions of a square. The models, however, are made with an element of abandon and ideas for the construction will often develop instinctively. I know that the chance shapes that appear are the language of the subconscious. Nevertheless, I am confident that I can impose an element of discipline on the model by the process of painting it and the knowledge that it has a basic form. The model for *Two circling butterflies* [page 54] broke up after the painting was finished. This impermanence was in itself significant as I wanted to suggest the ephemeral quality and frailty of the flight of two butterflies. As the brief touch of a bee collecting pollen, lasting a fraction of a second, can activate new growth, so a model that soon disintegrates can activate the beginning and completion of a painting.

I begin the painting when the model, conceived as a painting, is complete. The end is the beginning.

She knew how to hit to a hair's breadth that moment of the evening when the light and darkness are so evenly balanced that the constraint of the day and the suspense of the night neutralise each other, leaving absolute liberty.

Thomas Hardy
Tess of the d'Urbervilles

The paintings that you are looking at are about my involvement in the space of the landscape. The landscape has always been important for me, and I believe that hidden somewhere in it is a pattern of elemental and life-giving harmonies of proportion and colour. It is a search for this pattern that motivates the beginning of each painting.

From the introduction to an exhibition
Space and Light at the Barbican Centre 1991

Via Barbacarne

1949, gouache on paper
This was the first painting that I completed in the open, during an early visit to Italy.

A view from the greenhouse

1957, oil on canvas
Looking out from a transparent room towards Valley Cottage.

A rocking chair and bedroom slippers

1964, oil on canvas
The inside of the room can also be seen from the outside.

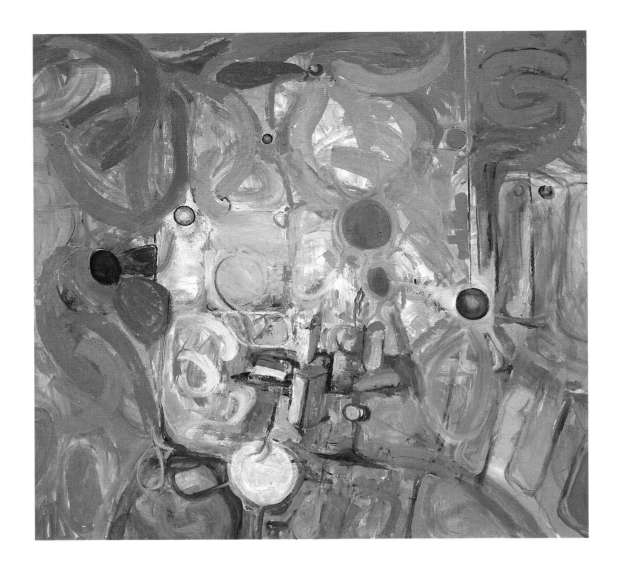

A disordered room

1965, oil on canvas
Points in the total space have been marked by hanging spheres and fruit on the table.

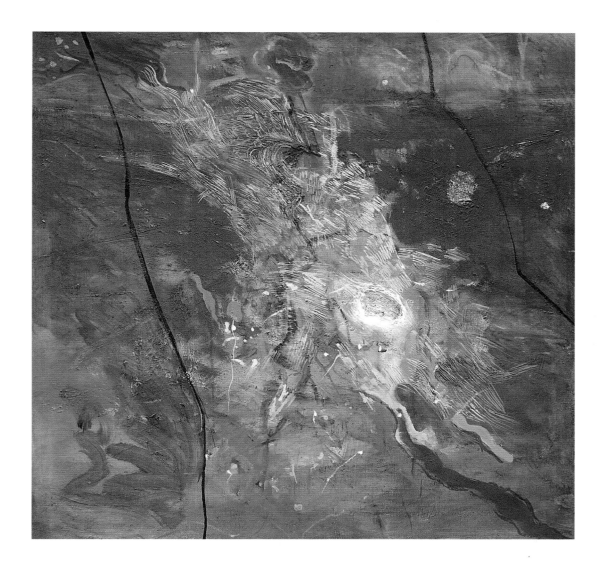

The birth of Aphrodite

1966, oil on canvas. Gaea ordered her son Cronus to castrate his father.
The genitals were thrown into the sea producing a white foam from which Aphrodite appeared.

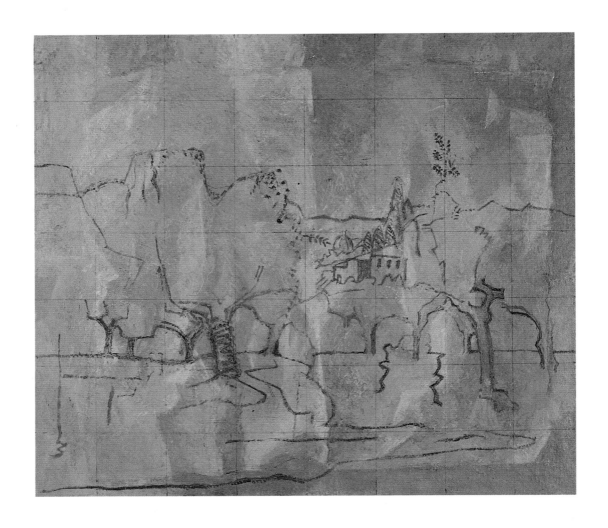

A fragment of gold from Tuscany

1976, oil on canvas
The outline of Florence, originally imprinted on a frail surface, becomes a fleeting memory.

A study. Wind moving over water

1983, gouache and ink on paper
Painted from a model made out of clay of the surface shapes of the water that are formed by the wind.

In the heat of midday

1978, pencil, ink and watercolour on paper
A drawing of olive trees is superimposed on expanding lines.

44

Light falling on water

1983, oil on canvas
Luminous discs lie behind the surface movement of the water.

Luminous mandala

1989, oil on canvas
Whichever way the dots are counted they always add up to 15.

Spanish bullfight

1990, oil on canvas. After a journey through a vast landscape of cornfields and contrasts
I saw a dead bull being dragged across the screen of a telvision.

Bluebell wood

1994, oil on canvas. The colour of the bluebells seems to float through the columns of trees as bursts of sunlight penetrate the green of the new beech leaves.

A piazza in Siena

1989, oil on canvas. This is a painting that suggests the space and atmosphere of the early Sienese paintings, the architecture of the city and the surrounding landscape.

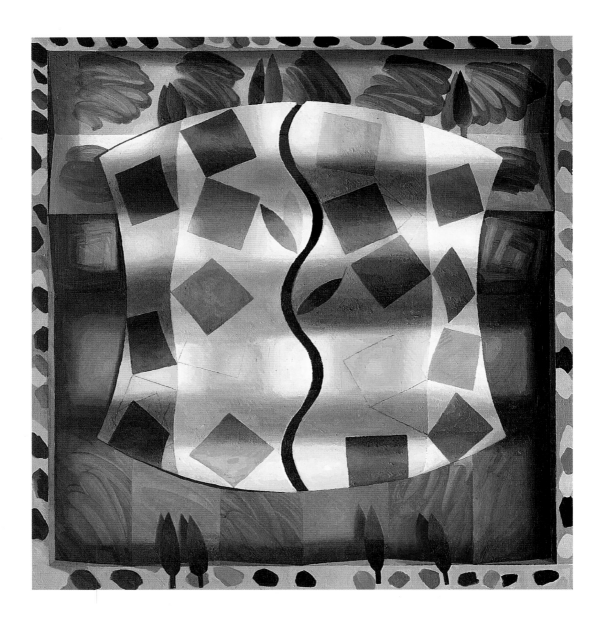

A Tuscan pageant

1990, oil on canvas
The coloured flags of Castel del Piano unfurl against the landscape as they are thrown up against the sky.

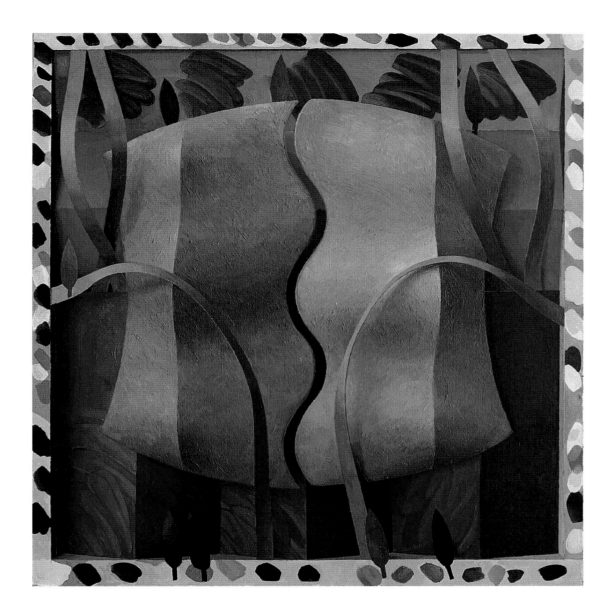

A Tuscan legend

1989, oil on canvas. Strong forms of the Tuscan hills fortify the outline of an ancient olive tree and somewhere among the roots lies the breastplate of a mediaeval warrior.

The cowpath walk

1990, oil on canvas. I have a favourite walk that leads from my studio up a valley and then along a cowpath above the folding hills and back again.

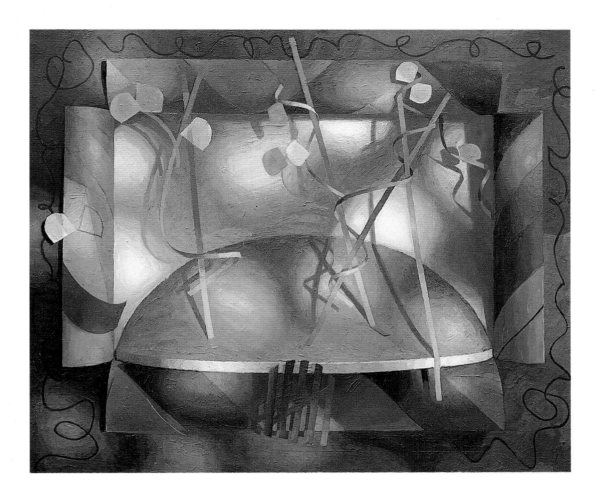

Sweet peas at Valley Cottage

1992, oil on canvas. The sweet peas bind themselves into a curtain that opens to reveal the old garden gate and rounded hillside. As the flowers unfurl and dance the light increases.

Two circling butterflies

1991, oil on canvas. Two butterflies circle around each other, never touching, and trace a line across the valley.
A relationship between the permanence of the hills and the transience of the butterflies.

Singing blackbird

1990, oil on canvas
The warm song of the blackbird shone from the centre of a sunlit garden throughout the summer.

Picking blackcurrants I

1990, oil on canvas. The idea for this painting came as my arms followed the
morning sun into a bush of ripening fruit.

Picking blackcurrants II

1990, oil on canvas
The colour of ripening fruit in the fading evening light.

Clouds above a landlocked sea

1992, oil on canvas
The movement of water is contained by the surrounding rocks.

A harbour

1994, oil on canvas
Rigid masts of sailing boats balance on the moving water.

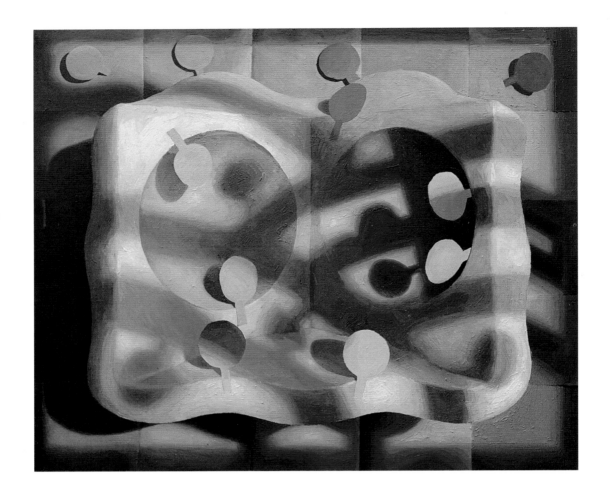

Landscape with opening seed pod

1990, oil on canvas. This painting began with the idea that the landscape seemed to germinate from seeds that were thrown from a bursting pod.

Cherry tree amongst layers of light

1992, oil on canvas
The form of the hillside, floating between the blossom and the sunlight, is remade in the shape of the tree.

Picking mushrooms. Early morning

1994, oil on canvas
Within the folds of the hills are white spots. They are hidden in the grass and wait to be discovered.

Picking mushrooms. Early evening

1994, oil on canvas. The shadows cast by the evening sun change the form of the mushroom field.
The white spots are harder to discover.

The stained glass of Bourges Cathedral

1995, oil on board. From the outside these windows seem dull, but seen from inside the colours burn.
I projected a strong light onto a model made out of clay.

San Biagio, Montepulciano

1993, oil on board. The brilliant sunlight from outside seemed to penetrate the walls
and then fill the dark interior.

Water flowing through trees

1995, oil on canvas. Walking along the banks of the river Teigne I was interested in the contrast between the continuous flowing movement of the water and the standing trees.

A wave in summer

1991, oil on canvas. The same pulse and counter movement of a wave generated in water
also seems to pass through the seasons.

Inside the Pantheon

1997, linocut. The opening at the top of the dome is halfway between
the chaos of infinity outside and the order inside.

An orange grove

1987, oil on canvas. From the Greek town of Leonidion a path leads to the sea through a fertile plain with dense shadows cast from orange trees.

Venice

1997, oil on canvas. The composition and the clarity of the light reflected on the water and buildings was inspired by the paintings of Carpaccio in the Academia.

Looking towards Monte Giove

1997, oil on board
A pine tree surrounds fragments of ancient walls in the Tuscan hills.

Sir Bryan Cartledge

1996, oil on canvas
Commissioned by Linacre College, Oxford.

When Linacre College selected Benedict to paint my portrait on my retirement as Principal, we arranged to meet at the College to give him an opportunity to absorb its atmosphere and geography, and to discuss practicalities. The first question to be settled was where the six one-hour sittings should take place and we quickly agreed that on grounds of light and freedom from interruption his own studio, rather than my study in Linacre, was preferred. This was a decision that I never regretted. Benedict lives in a delightful rambling cottage tucked into a narrow, secluded valley of the Chilterns. It is full of atmosphere and memories. Bendict's studio is at the back of the house, overlooking the garden and flooded in a north light through large windows and a partially glazed roof. It is full of work in progress, in various media and styles, which engages a sitter's eye; the garden, equally, gives a sitter plenty to watch, not least the antics of a pair of predatory magpies. Boredom was never a problem.

Benedict attaches importance to using the background of a portrait to place the subject in the context of his or her life, or at least to suggest its salient themes. Benedict proposed, and I agreed, that Russia, which had been the main focus of my earlier diplomatic career, might be suggested by a model of an onion-domed church. This was placed on a table at my elbow. (It was Tessa, his wife, who made the dome out of clay on her potter's wheel). A faint charcoal outline, on a folded sheet of paper like an architect's working drawing, represented Linacre's new building – the most visible legacy of my Principalship. Benedict seated me on a plain wooden chair, which turned out to be more comfortable than it looked.

I had been worried about the difficulty of remaining reasonably still for an hour at a time; but fidgeting usually results from boredom and, in addition to the interest provided by the physical surroundings of the studio, Benedict himself provided a great deal to occupy the eye and the mind as he set to work. I was, for example, fascinated by a device of his own invention which had been inspired, he told me, by a less sophisticated tool used by Dürer. Benedict's improved version consists of a frame, fitted on to the easel where the canvas would normally be, into which he slides a sheet of glass; extended from the easel towards the artist are two supports holding a small piece of wood in which an aperture has been cut. The artist looks through the aperture, and thence through the glass, at the subject and 'traces' the outline of the sitter on to the glass with a felt pen. This enables him to fix the position of the head and body, and the proportions of, for example, head to hands, and subsequently to copy his preferred choice of several versions on to the canvas via tracing paper. This whole process provides plenty of visual interest for the sitter. The early sittings usually concluded with a session in which photographs were taken, on a large format camera, to provide further raw material for his work on the portrait between sittings. And, of course, we talked. As a devoted music-lover with memories of singing several of Edmund Rubbra's choral compositions in choirs at school and at Cambridge,

I was fascinated by Benedict's reminiscences of his father and his father's contemporaries. Far from being relieved when the the final sitting came to an end, I felt real regret that the sessions and my visits to Valley Cottage were over; but the insights which they gave me into the art and techniques of the portrait painter remain and help me, I find, to look at portraits with a slightly more informed eye than I could before.

Sir Bryan Cartledge, KCMG, MA, 1997

PORTRAITS

I believe that the eyes are the focal point of the portrait. It is through the eyes that we enter into the character of the person. The portrait should be direct and the likeness made unequivocal through the understanding of form and the careful consideration of the general pose, the tip and the turn of the head, the position of the hands and placing of the figure in the canvas.

The colour and shapes of the background are chosen to enhance the 'feel' of the person and to emphasise the movement of the pose. These elements bring the portrait to life.

The portrait should speak, through the gestures of the sitter and the choice of clothes, of a timeless quality. As the photograph records a fleeting moment, the portrait should cover a broader time scale. (Written for a client in 1990)

My mother and father and brother used to sit for me and in turn I would sit for my aunt Elizabeth. At school Nell persuaded David Herbert, my English teacher, to pose for his portrait. We became good friends and later, in his capacity as a publisher, he commissioned me to write two books, both entitled *Painting Children*. The first was for Studio Vista in 1968 and the second, twenty-five years later, was published by his own Herbert Press. The Studio Vista publication coincided with the conception of my idea to build a studio and gallery. My aim was to have a career both as a painter and as a portraitist. I wanted these two aspects of painting to run along parallel lines and as a result of my book and a brochure that I had printed this became possible. The income from the portrait commissions gave me the freedom to develop my ideas about landscapes, space and light.

The two sides of my painting began to interact. By painting my constructions that are, in a sense, already the finished painting, I can interrupt ongoing work in favour of a commission without losing the line of continuity. The constant light and forms of the model can wait until the portrait is finished. There is also a relationship between the model making and the way the backgrounds of the portraits are considered and painted. The design of the colours and shapes that surround the figure, as important as the figure itself, is independently constructed. When I am satisfied that the design and

Antoinette Rubbra. The artist's mother

1973, oil on board

colours relate to and augment the figure, this 'background' is observed and painted as an integral part of the portrait.

Each commission presents a new challenge and each one must be resolved satisfactorily from mine and from the client's point of view. I have evolved a system that has become a framework within which I can experiment and express myself freely. The composition and pose is established with the tracings from my 'drawing machine', described by Sir Bryan Cartledge (see page 73), and the work done during the six sittings is often changed and then finally resolved away from the sitter. Selected details of photographs are used to position and help observe continually changing forms: the folds in the clothes, the flow of the hair and sometimes the expression. If I have to travel to the sitter I arrive armed with a white screen (to place behind the figure), comfortable chairs, a dais (to raise young children to my eye level) and white sheets to diffuse the sunlight. I also arrive, for the first sitting, with an air of confidence to disguise my initial apprehension.

Ursula Vaughan Williams

1984, oil on canvas. Commissioned by Charterhouse.

Violeta Ainslie

1991, oil on calico and board, detail

Teddy Craig

1981, oil on canvas

Martin Phipps

1982, oil on canvas

Judith Slater

1976, oil on board

The Hon. David Bathurst

1986, oil on canvas

Sir Maurice Dorman

1987, oil on canvas. Commissioned by The Most Venerable Order of the Hospital of St John of Jerusalem.
(The Order of St John)

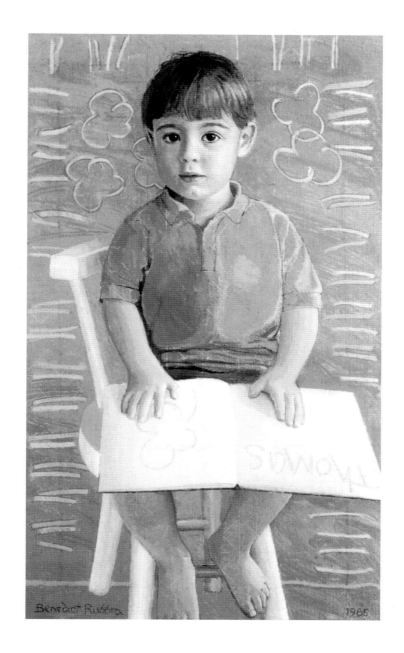

Thomas Richards

1985, oil on canvas

BENEDICT RUBBRA: BIOGRAPHY		
	1938–47	Childhood at Valley Cottage.1947. First of many influential visits to Florence in Italy.
	1947–56	School at Christ's Hospital. Encouraged by Nell Todd to study painting.
	1956–60	Studied at the Slade School of Fine Art. Influenced by the teaching of Patrick George. Exhibited with the Young Contemporaries.
	1961	Worked near Aix-en-Provence painting landscape.
	1962–63	Further travel and worked in Italy and Greece.
	1964	Married. Worked in London and part-time teaching at Oxford, High Wycombe and Horsham until 1970.
	1965	First one-man exhibition at Marlborough College.
	1966	First one-man exhibiton in London, Woodstock Gallery.
	1967	Moved from London to live and work at Valley Cottage.
	1968	One-man exhibition at Marlborough College.
	1970	Built a studio and gallery as an annex to Valley Cottage.
	1971	Set up as a portrait painter.
	1972	First exhibition at Valley Cottage. Exhibitions of portraits and paintings continued to be held here every two years.
	1978	Began the process of making models based on ideas drawn from the landscape that then become the starting point for the paintings.
	1979	One-man exhibition in London, Campbell and Franks.
	1980–84	Exhibited Royal Academy summer exhibitions.
	1985	Began a series of paintings based on the problems of drawing with light.
	1989	10th exhibition at Valley Cottage opened by Sir Oliver Millar.
	1991	Exhibition of paintings, Barbican Centre, London.
	1992	Exhibition of paintings, John Bly Antiques, St James's, London.
	1992	11th exhibition at Valley Cottage, opened by Sir Simon Gourlay.
	1994	12th exhibition at Valley Cottage.
	1995	Exhibited paintings and working model, City Museum, Hereford.
	1996	Working for six months in Venice and Rome.

Notable portrait commissions:

HRH The Prince of Wales
    for the Fishmongers' Company
Lord Hailsham
Sir Ove Arup
Dame Bridget D'Oyly Carte
Ursula Vaughan Williams
Sir Maurice Dorman
The Hon. David Bathhurst
Sir Colin Davis
Sir Maurice Bowra
Sir Simon Gourlay
Sir Charles Frossard
Sir Bryan Cartledge
Sir Terence English

Publications

Painting Children
    Studio Vista, London;
    Watson-Guptill New York, 1968
Draw Portraits
    Pitman, 1980
Painting Children
    The Herbert Press, London;
    Watson-Guptill, New York, 1993

Paintings with:

Nuffield Foundation
Contemporary Arts Association
Government Offices
Private collections in USA,
    Switzerland, and the UK